CONNECTING THE DOTS
TO FIND YOUR CALLING

Blessing
on your future –

Rory

Prov 3:5-6

CONNECTING THE DOTS TO FIND YOUR CALLING

BY

RANDY BRASHEARS

XULON PRESS

Xulon Press
2301 Lucien Way #415
Maitland, FL 32751
407.339.4217
www.xulonpress.com

Unless otherwise indicated, Scripture quotations taken from the Holy Bible, New International Version (NIV). Copyright © 1973, 1978, 1984, 2011 by Biblica, Inc.™. Used by permission. All rights reserved.

Printed in the United States of America.

ISBN-13: 978-1-54565-362-3

Acknowledgements

o o o

- My wife Kim and our sons, Jerome and William, for all their support during each of our moves along the East Coast.

- My father Robert, my mother Anna and my brother Rob, who valued family life in Aberdeen.

- My Christian brothers Irwin Overton and Mark Ware who have been faithful supporters over the years.

- The professional men and women of Law Enforcement.

- The Ministry of the Fellowship of Christian Peace Officers who provided encouragement and a platform to serve.

- Ret. LAPD Assistant Chief Bob Vernon and Chaplain Jack Crans who have been my role models for service.

- The Colson Fellows Program who sparked a love for reading.

- My Lord and Savior Jesus Christ who gave me my calling in life.

Introduction

o   o   o

Many young people today struggle with what to do with their lives. What is their calling and how do they find it? In this book we will look back over my career in law enforcement to see how God connected the dots through my past, my passion and my prospects to lay out the calling for my life.

As you think through your past, passion, and prospects, you too may find the divine calling that God has given you so that you may be fulfilled in this life and prepared for the next. So, pour yourself a cup of tea or coffee and let's get started.

Contents

o o o

CHAPTER 1:

In the Beginning
Along I- 95

o   o   o

The City of Aberdeen is located along I-95 in Harford County Maryland. My family moved there in the mid-1960's when I was a one year old. We lived in the community known as Swan Meadows. This neighborhood was made up of single family and duplex homes created in the 1940s as military housing. The community is located adjacent to the Aberdeen Proving Ground (APG) Military Base.

Our home on Liberty Street was a small single-family home consisting of two bedrooms and one bathroom in a cozy 672 square feet. Our backyard abutted the fence to APG property. Driving by the house as an adult made me ponder how we could fit in there so comfortably. To me, it looks like the space of a two and a half car garage.

I was born to the parents of Robert and Anna Brashears. They were both elementary school teachers. I had one sibling, Rob, who was eighteen months my senior.

APG is one of the Army's oldest active Proving Grounds. One of their major missions was to test ordinances. Yes, they would blow things up, and it wasn't unusual for one of their tests to gently shake our home. But just like people who live along railroad tracks, you soon get used to the noise and think nothing of it.

My parents taught several towns over which meant that they would have to leave for work prior to us leaving for school. And we would get home in the afternoon prior to my parent's arrival. My brother and I walked to the Halls Cross Road Elementary School. Back in those days, neighbors kept a watchful eye out for each other's kids.

The closest call to trouble that I recall is when I was in the third grade and my brother and I decided to

2

take up smoking. Our father was a smoker and he would have cigarette butts in the ashtray. We would lite up the remainder of the cigarette butt. On one occasion, while sitting on our living room couch and having a smoke, the remaining tip of the lit cigarette dropped away from the filter and on to the couch. I watched it burn a hole in the couch cover and fall into the couch itself. Fearing a couch fire, I began to beat the couch to put out the smoldering remains of the cigarette. It worked. Now there was the little problem, a hole in the couch cover. After consulting with my brother, we decided to rearrange the cover to hide the hole. This seemed to work and that was the end of our experimentation with smoking.

Chapter 2:

Kid Cop

o o o

My brother and I walked about one mile to attend Halls Cross Road Elementary school. The Principal at that time was Mr. Mears. He was a caring older gentleman that the students and faculty loved. He carried a little leather strap. This was back in the days of corporal punishment in the public schools. I found it a little odd that as Mr. Mears would walk around the school, some of the kids would hold out their hands to him so that he could give them a friendly tap on the hand with his strap.

I didn't want any part of that. Our father had a simple rule. If either one of us had to get spanked in school, we would surely get another one when we got home. This was back in the day when most parents supported the authority structures of society and expected their children to do the same. Needless to say, my brother and I never received a spanking in school.

I do recall one day when the Vice Principal carried out his corporal punishment duties. What made this unique is that he did it in the office with an open mic to the schools PA system. Needless to say, the children in the entire school were on their best behavior for weeks to come. Today that would be called psychological abuse or something of that nature.

One of my favorite memories of elementary school was that I was a member of the School Safety Patrol. Yes, this was the first badge of authority that I had ever worn. Our primary mission was to raise and lower the US Flag in front of the school each day and to monitor the lobby and hallways in the morning. Our goal was to keep kids from running in the halls.

To assist with the goal of speed enforcement through the halls of the school, I invented human "radar". The entrance hall ran adjacent to the gym.

So, I came up with the plan to increase our capture of hall running violators. I posted a fellow Safety Patrol member inside the gym but where he could secretly observe the lobby and detect any violators. If he saw one, he would yell to me across the gym that one was coming and give a brief description of the runner. I would then step out of the other gym door in front of the offender and bust them for running in the hall.

This worked well until our radar operation was halted by a member of the faculty. They preferred a visual deterrence over speed enforcement.

Across the street from the school was a field that would collect water and freeze over in the winter. Kids would hang out there and slide around on the ice before class. But as you can imagine, with young kids having fun, the time would get away from them and they would be late. On several occasions I recall being dispatched across the street to round up the delinquent students and bring them on to school. Little did I know that these activities were setting the seeds of future law enforcement service in my heart.

Right next to the school there was a little convenience store called SIDS Market. Although I do not recall actually witnessing this, I believed that some of our students engaged in shoplifting after school. I dreamt about taking my badge off of the safety vest, putting it in my wallet and staking out the store to bust some shoplifters. Fortunately for all involved, it was just a dream and I never acted on the idea.

During my final year at Hall Cross Road Mr. Mears retired. We got a new principal who wasn't a big fan of the School Safety Patrol except for flag duties. That was a shame, but it was time to move on to my next school.

My next stop was Aberdeen Middle School. This school was across town so I had to ride the school bus. The school opened in 1973 and I began attending in 1974. It was a nice building but in some ways was run like a prison. I realize that the middle school years can be very challenging but some things just didn't set right with me. For example, we had a male principal and a female vice principal. I observed each make routine inspections of the opposite gender bathrooms during the course of the day. On more than one occasion I was using the urinal in the boys' room to have the female vice principal walk in and stand there. This just seemed to me at the time to be something that happens in correctional facilities.

Our school had a field to the rear that backed up to woods. I observed my teacher in high heeled shoes take off running out of our classroom door to run down a student who was trying to "escape" from the school and head for the woods. To my surprise, they would often catch them and bring them back.

My time in Middle School went well overall but there were some school bullies to contend with. I tried to avoid them as much as possible. During this time, like with many young men, I was a fan of professional wrestling. I would watch it every Saturday afternoon on TV. I then learned about the community Parks and Recreation Wrestling program. I signed up. Having no clue about the physical training level needed to wrestle, I attended the first session totally cold.

I made it through the two hours work out, came home, and laid on my bed to sleep. When I woke up, nothing would move except my eyelids. I rolled out of bed and was sore from my head to my feet!! I could barely walk. To make matters worse, the gym class I was currently taking was a class called conditioning. We were to jump over things, pull up on a rope, etc. I could barely walk from the weekends wrestling and I had to tell the teacher that I couldn't participate.

Soon all the training and conditioning helped build the necessary self-confidence to handle myself. I realized that bullies will continue to bully unless confronted. There was a boy in school who would push me around a little. I also saw him take lunch tickets from other boys. It was then that I decided that he was no longer going to get away with putting his hands on me. Now I realized that he was bigger and stronger than me. We shared a metal shop class together. So, I had picked out which tool I would use to part his skull the next time he put his hands on me. I knew I needed a little advantage in the battle so the element of surprise and a foot long metal file would do the trick. Fortunately for him and me, he didn't touch me again.

One of the incidents that stick out the most in my mind is my seventh-grade science class. During the class, there was a student, Billy Bad Boy, who was acting up in class. The teacher, who tried to control him, grew more and more frustrated with his disruptions. Finally, she had had enough. She whipped out her referral document and scribbled out the charges for this "arrest warrant". She then told Billy Bad Boy to report to the office. She then quickly looked over the class and ordered me to hand carry the "warrant" to the office and escort Billy there. I complied.

As I walked Billy to the office, neither one of us opened the rolled-up document to read about the charges. We arrived at the office and I handed over Billy and the referral to the Principal's secretary. It would be years later that I would reflect back on that day to see that the seeds of law enforcement were planted deeper within me.

Probably the most influential moment of Middle School occurred when we had career day. We had a visitor from the Maryland Natural Resources Police Department. He, in full uniform, spoke about his job. He talked about enforcing hunting laws in the woods and oyster fishing laws on the water. While I wasn't too interested in working in the woods or on the water, I was interested in the gun on his hip. (Remember I was a middle school boy). This began to open up my mind to a career in law enforcement. Within six months, I learned about an organization that the Lord would use to change my life.

Chapter 3:

Explorer Post 9020

o o o

One of my senventh-grade class mates was Fran Farley. I am not sure how the conversation came up, but she told me about the Aberdeen Police Department's Law Enforcement Explorer Post. Her father was Cpl. Frank Farley and he was the advisor to the group.

Law Enforcement Explorers are groups made up of students aged fourteen to twenty one. They are chartered by the Boy Scouts of America and they are sponsored by local law enforcement agencies. I was very excited to hear about this group. I applied and was accepted. The year was 1975. Within two years I became Captain of the Post.

Some of the things that we did were:

- Assist with Traffic Control and Parking at the annual Armed Forces Day at APG

- Assist with Traffic Control and Parking at the annual Boat Regatta Race in Havre de Grace, MD

- Assist with the Traffic Control at the annual Fourth of July Parade

- Hand out our crime prevention literature

- Work the Dispatch Desk

- Participate in Ride-a-longs with the City Police

I was able to log in many hours working dispatch. I would receive emergency calls over the telephone and dispatch officers to handle the calls. Once I became proficient, the on-duty dispatcher could sit back and let me handle his or her job. As I look back on it, that was a lot of responsibility for a teenager.

I recall one night answering the phone and it was a caller who was threatening suicide. I told the on-duty dispatcher but he didn't take over the call. So, I continued and obtained the address of the caller. It turns out that it was just outside our city limits. I wrote down the address and asked the dispatcher to call the Sheriffs Dept to respond to the address. I felt it was appropriate to stay on the line until they arrive. So, I switched phones to another room so I could continue to talk to the caller and free up the main phone for the dispatcher to resume control of the desk. I continued to talk to the caller until the Harford County Sheriff Deputy arrived on the scene. I returned to the front desk and resumed taking calls and dispatching police.

As interesting and important as the dispatch center, was participating in the Ride-A-Longs is where I was truly bitten by the law enforcement bug. I did this throughout my years in high school. One of the hoodlums in our city sent word that if he ever caught me trying to arrest anyone he would bust me in the head with a bottle. I kept this in mind...

After graduating from High School, I attended Harford Community College and studied Criminal

Justice. We were encouraged to select a minor but I couldn't think of one. By this time all I knew was criminal justice. I began attending sessions of the District Court to monitor traffic and criminal cases. I continue to participate in the Ride-A-Long program.

The call to serve in the criminal justice field had been fully set. The next decision was to decide where to serve.

Chapter 4:

Seasonal Service

o o o

My first paycheck from a police depart-ment came in 1983 from the Maryland Toll Facilities Police where I was employed as a Seasonal (Summer) Dispatcher. The location was the Susquehanna River Bridge. The name was later changed to the Thomas J. Hatem Memorial Bridge. The bridge is a four-lane, one point four-mile structure that was built in 1940. The bridge spans the Susquehanna River on U.S. Route 40 between the towns of Havre de Grace, Maryland and Perryville, Maryland. Adjacent to this bridge is a parallel bridge that crosses that same river on I-95.

Each summer they hire two seasonal dispatchers to cover the day and evening shifts Monday through Friday. My prior experience as a Law

Enforcement Explorer Scout with many hours of dispatching under my belt came in handy.

The dispatch office overlooks the Toll Plaza where the toll money is collected. The job, as you might expect, was routine with not a lot of action. The day that sticks out in my mind was a dayshift assignment. Cpl. Nichols was the shift commander and Officers Presnell, Pyles, and Moses were on duty. Cpl. Nichols and Officer Moses left the area to respond to the agency Headquarters in Baltimore. This was about forty-five minutes to an hour south of the Hatem Bridge.

The shift was quiet when I received a report of a male subject acting strange and about to cross the Bridge on foot. Pedestrians and bikes were not allowed on the bridge as there was no shoulder for them to safely cross. I dispatched Officer Presnell to the call. Because our large bay window overlooked the Toll Plaza, I could see the suspect in question. He was a black male in his 20's. Officer Presnell called enroute. I then called Officer Pyles to assist. "Susquehanna to 618". I got no response. I called again, "Susquehanna 618". Again, I got no response. I tried a third time but louder on the radio. No response. Officer Presnell attempted to reach his partner, "615 to 618". No response. Officer Presnell arrived at the scene and begin speaking with the individual. I could see that the subject was starting to get agitated and begin to swing his arms in the air as he tried to walk passed the officer and head to the bridge. I had a sick feeling that this wasn't going to end well. Officer Presnell was a very good and proactive officer. But he was one of the smallest officers on the force. Officer Pyles, on the other hand, was the opposite of proactive and one of the largest. I remember looking at the display case in the dispatch office that contained several nightsticks. The thought crossed my mind to grab the stick, abandon my desk, sprint across the Toll Plaza and back him up myself. I then saw what I believed to be an off-duty or unmarked State Police Car about to enter the Toll Plaza. I grabbed a portable radio and ran out on the steps and tried to get his attention without success. I could look across the Plaza and see that the disorderly subject was getting closer to the beginning of the bridge. I then thought about calling the neighboring police agency for assistance. I ran back into the office and called the

Havre de Grace Police Dispatcher. The Dispatcher sent two units to the rescue.

I attempted again to raise Officer Pyles. This time he answered the radio and said he would respond to back up his partner. As I watched and waited the disorderly subject was close to entering the travel lane on the bridge. It was then that I saw one of the best sights in life. Two Havre de Grace Police Units cresting the hill of the bridge with lights and sirens to the rescue. They were able to deal with the subject and get him off the bridge. Officer Pyles did show up, once everything was done....

After the incident was over, I called back the dispatcher at Havre de Grace and thanked them for their assistance. Because Havre de Grace was across the river and in another county, the call was a long-distance call. We had to log all long-distance calls in our log book. Later that afternoon when Cpl. Nichols returned to the station, he was standing next to me and looking at the log book. He saw two calls the Havre de Grace Police and asked about them. I told him what had happened while he was gone. Then Officer Pyles walked in and Cpl. Nichols lit into him. Officer Pyles was trying to blame the condition of the police car for not being able to drive fast enough. It was embarrassing to watch so I picked up the portable radio and left the dispatch so that he could be counseled in private.

One Friday night after my seasonal employment ended, I stopped by the Police Office to see who was working. It was Officer Moses and he was working alone that evening. So, as we were visiting, he was notified of a pledge. A pledge was a person who has crossed the bridge but didn't have the money to pay the toll. The operator was directed into the police office where their license status was checked, and they would sign a pledge to pay the toll later.

As I was seated in the dispatch chair, Officer Moses was in the next room with the pledge. Everything seemed normal, but I began to get a sense from God that I was to leave. I didn't want to be rude and leave without finishing our visit, but the impression became stronger to leave immediately. So, I got up, told Officer Moses that I had to go and left. It was weeks later that I learned that the pledge was in the possession of a loaded firearm and once discovered by the officer, was placed under arrest. This was one of my first of many lessons that when God told me about a tactical situation, I had better listen.

The next summer I learned about another seasonal position, but his time as a sworn police officer. The location was the Town of Ocean City, MD.

Ocean City is an Atlantic resort town located in Worcester County, Maryland. The year-round population is approximately 7,000 people. The population during the summer can rise to over 300,000 people making Ocean City the second largest municipality in the State of Maryland.

The south end of town is known for its famous three-mile-long Boardwalk. Mid-town is known for dining, nightlife and the north end has high rise condominiums.

Because of this growth in population, the Towns police force must expand for the summer season. In the 80's, the town would hire as many as one-hundred Seasonal Police Officers to patrol the nine-mile Island from the Inlet to the Delaware line.

I applied for the Seasonal Officer Position and was hired. I believe that my experience as an Explorer Scout and a Dispatcher allowed me to do very well on the interview. I recall that we could be assigned to one of three divisions: Vehicle Patrol, Foot Patrol on the Boardwalk, or Foot Patrol downtown. At the end of my interview, Captain Dave Massey asked me where I wanted to work. I replied, "Vehicle Patrol" and he said OK.

After completing a two-week police academy consisting of twleve-hour days, I was assigned to Officer Jan Jones for field training. I recall several officers on the shift asking me who my FTO was and when I said Jan Jones, I would get a snicker or a roll of the eyes. I later learned that Jan was old school and a little rough around the edges but that is exactly what I needed. I already knew how to be nice to people, especially when they were being cooperative with me. But I needed some training on dealing with people who were not so nice or cooperative and God put me with the right man for the job.

While on patrol one evening we got a call to a high-rise condo. The complainant was a group of females who were being harassed by a group of males in another condo. They were all high school aged students. I recall as we were leaving the girls unit to speak to the guys, one of the girls instructed us to give them a good scare. I chuckled out loud as we left their unit. I told my FTO that we can't go around violating people's rights……

We arrived at the suspects unit and Jan Jones pounded rather loudly on the door and ended with a kick on the door with his boot. He had my attention. A young man answered the door and Jan told them that we needed to talk to them about what had occurred. Once inside he ordered everyone to sit down. There were about five guys in the unit. All complied except one. I suspect he had been drinking. Officer Jones told him to sit down but the young man refused. His friends were pleading with him to sit down but he ignored them as well. Here I was watching my FTO and the young man standing nose to nose in a standoff.

At that point, I placed my report folder on the counter and joined Officer Jones by standing inches away from the subject's face at a right angle. I hoped the additional bluff would work.

It did, and he sat down. Officer Jones then addressed the complaint with the young men and told them under no uncertain terms were they to harass the young ladies in the other unit. We then left and continued patrol. This incident helped me realize the community caretaking / parental supervision aspects of policing. Sometimes you just have to give what is called the police look to let a youthful offender know that I see what you are doing, and I do not like it. Usually, that is enough to change most bad behavior without a word of counseling or formal action.

After the completion of my field training program, I began to patrol Sector four. The town was divided into five patrol sectors. Each was staffed with a Seasonal Police Officer. The Full-Time Officers served in overlapping sectors so that they could be our primary back up on most calls.

The North end of the town was made up of high rises and was a little more family-oriented. Therefore, our tolerance for noise and disturbances was a little lower than the South end of town that had more bars and pedestrian activities.

My first arrest came as a result of a detail. They were having problems in the South end with beer being stolen from delivery trucks while deliveries were being made. They asked for two volunteers to work plain clothes to monitor the deliveries. I volunteered. We even used our own vehicles.

While conducting surveillance, I didn't see any activity around the beer truck but I observed two elementary aged boys ride by on a bike. The boy riding on the back of the bike was excited as he held up an adult porn magazine. I thought who in the world would sell an adult magazine to boys that young? So, I fired up the car and begin to follow them. I got them stopped on the Board Walk and I radioed my location to the dispatcher. I then asked the boys who sold them the magazine. They replied, "No one, we stole it". After learning where the theft had occurred, I placed both boys under arrest. At the station, I placed my first of many hundred calls to a parent informing them that their child has been arrested. The mother worked in a bank and had to leave work and responded to the station. She was very cooperative but fit to be tied at her son. I quietly gave her some advice. I told her that I could see that she is very upset so a good strategy, once they get into the car, is to say nothing, cool down, speak to her husband when he gets home and approach their son on a unified front. She thanked me for the advice. A full-time officer who overheard our conversation told me that was good advice. I learned this from my own mother when I did something very stupid as a child in a store.

We rotated shifts every two weeks. My favorite shift was midnights. The air was cool, and the alcohol was flowing. I had heard many stories about some of the crazy fights that took place and just how busy it could be but the summer of 1984 was relatively mild. The worst fight that my shift was involved in occurred on my day off. I remember our sergeant reprimanding some of the officers in roll call the following day for NOT using their night-sticks during the big brawl.

My summer at the beach ended and I returned to college for my final year. During this time of my life, my goal was to be a federal agent. After graduating from the University of Baltimore with a BS Degree in Criminal Justice, I sought oppor-tunities to get into the federal system. My first job as a fed was with the Federal Protective Service in Maryland. Although this was a law enforcement position, it was more like a glorified security guard. I was bored out of my mind. Six months later I obtained a position with the Defense Investigative Service. In this position, we assisted field agents to conduct background investigations on military and DOD Civilians.

This job was the opposite of boring. It was very high pressured and the workflow was continuous even on your day off.

During my time there, I took two exams for Federal Law Enforcement positions. Each promised that they would have the results in six to eight weeks. I waited eight weeks, ten weeks, then twleve weeks and no results. I began to pray about where God really wanted me to work.

On the home front, I needed to get closer to my job, so I moved to Howard County, Md. into a town-house with three other housemates. On my first day there, one of my housemates invited me to attend a social event in Baltimore County. He was going to spend the night there, but I would drive back to my new home. After the event, I begin heading home on I-83 south which went from Baltimore County into Baltimore City. Just prior to entering the city, my car broke down. I was able to make it to the shoulder of the road. This was the time before cell phones. Because it was near two jurisdictions, it was a no man's land when it came to police patrols. So, I sat and waited.

Since I had just moved out from home, my mother didn't know my whereabouts and because I had just moved in with some housemates that I have yet to meet, they wouldn't be looking for me either. I was alone. As the hours went by I drifted off to sleep. I was awoken to the headlights of a car who had pulled off the road behind me. Two guys got out their car and approached my car. Once they got a little closer and realized that the car was occupied, they stopped in their tracks, turned around and took off. I realized then that they were not there to help but to steal.

While stuck there I began to realize that I didn't care what fancy investigations the Feds were doing. I needed a cop. I begin to appreciate the routine duties of the police officer from the point of view of the public. The Assist Motorist Call wasn't glamorous but very important. I thought back on the times in which I had done that in Ocean City or while riding with the Aberdeen Police Department. I saw this function in a new light.

Eventually, a tow truck stopped to check on me and I was rescued. But God used the incident to begin turning my heart from being a Federal Agent to being a local police officer. The other thing God used was seeing a police car running lights and siren pass me. I missed that in Ocean City. I finally said OK. I asked God that if He wanted me to be in local policing to show me which Department. I didn't want to throw out six applications and see which one took. Through a series of circumstances, He pointed me to the Baltimore County, Maryland Police Department.

Here are some interesting facts:

- In April 1874, the Baltimore County Police Department was formed.

- In 1885, the first call boxes were installed

- In 1916, the first police car was purchased

- In 1930, forty-eight Officers were employed

- In 1952, the first African American Officers were hired

- In 1974, the first female Officer was placed on patrol

- In 1985, Baltimore County Police receives National Accreditation

- In 1989, Baltimore County Police is the first major police agency and the second in the nation to receive reaccreditation

- In 2008, Baltimore County Police had ten Police stations, 848 vehicles, 1900 sworn Officers, three boats, three helicopters, twenty-eight K-9 dogs, nine Police Athletic Centers, and six motorcycles. (Baltimore County police Department 135th Anniversary Book).

The Baltimore County Police Department was a large and professional organization that I didn't know much about. Since I grew up in Harford County, I didn't have much exposure to Baltimore County but that is where the Lord pointed me to, so I applied.

The last hurdle for the application process was the physical exam. I knew that my eyesight had changed from all that desk work at the Defense Department, so I went and had my eyes checked and my prescription updated for my glasses. While in the doctor's office, I asked the doctor what my uncorrected vision was. He told me and asked why I needed that information. I said it was for a job. He asked me what the standard was, and I said twenty forty. He replied, "You will never make it".

I left the office feeling very dejected. On the one hand, I wanted God to close this door if this wasn't the right department for me, but everything up to this point told me that it was. On the week of my official county physical, I attended a prayer meeting at our local church. My intent was to ask the congregation to pray for me and my appointment the next day. But as I sat and listened to the songs that were sung in this old-time, southern gospel church, I heard themes like: God can do whatever he wants to do.

I felt encouraged and went to my appointment the following day. The last item in the exam was the eye test. The Doctor took me into the hall and pulled down the eye chart. She said read line three. I couldn't see line three. She repeated the command. I thought at that point I didn't have anything else to lose so I guessed at what I was seeing. I was so far off she thought I was reading the wrong line. She barked at me to read line three. I then said a simple prayer, "Help me, Jesus." Suddenly something popped in my eyes and I could read the chart. I was stunned.

Then, I said to myself, "Fool, read the chart"! I read the line out loud and my eyes popped back to normal. I passed the physical and entered the Baltimore County Police Academy. I was afraid to tell that story for about the first ten years of my career for fear that first, people wouldn't believe it and second, they might make me retake the eye test again!

Chapter 5:

Police Academy

o   o   o

In the 1980's the Baltimore County Police
Academy was located in a former elementary school in a residential neighborhood located
in Dundalk Maryland. On October 15, 1987,
the Academy Staff hosted a family orientation
day before the start of the academy. This gave
spouses, parents and recruit officers the opportunity to see where the recruits would be spending
the next six months of their lives. The staff was very
friendly and polite. There were two of my fellow
recruits who showed up a little late for the orientation. One made the off the cuff remark about
being "fashionably late." The staff laughed it off. I
had a sick feeling that we had not heard the last
of that remark. The staff asked if there were any
questions. One recruit raised his hand and asked

about the snow policy. The Sergeant smiled and said, "Did you see the flagpole out in front of the building? Well if the snow piles up to the top of the flagpole, then the academy will be closed." His final comment was to thank the families for coming and for the recruits to try not to be late on Monday morning at seven thirty AM.

The seventy-sixth Recruit Class began on Monday, October 17, 1987. We all arrived in sports jackets and ties and began by standing in formation in the academy gym. At some point, one of the Sergeants reminded us of the comment made by the recruit on orientation day. They also explained what an AA session was. No, it wasn't where we would sit in a small group, use only our first names, and admit to our addictions and hang-ups. This AA stood for attitude adjustment, and we were about to get our first one.

The Sergeant yelled for everyone to get on the floor in the push-up position and hold it for further instructions. We then did pushups. We were back on our feet and being yelled at for everything under the sun. It was a warm day in October and the gym was hot.

This activity went on for a while and then it happened. A recruit passed out. In a little while, another one hit the floor. It is kind of hard to help your partner when you are standing at attention. They then yelled at us for passing out and hitting the floor. The Sergeant said if you are going to pass out, then go down to one knee.

Back then in the 80's Baltimore County Officers wore white shirts. I watched the Sergeant's pace back and forth. Something very strange started to happen. I had never seen it before or since. Black dots appeared on the Sergeant's shirt. As he walked back and forth in front of us, the dots got larger. His white shirt was turning black in front of my eyes. I thought to myself, I think I am about to pass out. But I do not want to be one of them. But I do not want to smash my face on the floor either. I fought it for a while then went to a knee.

The Sergeant took two or three of us who were kneeling outside to get fresh air. My eyesight immediately returned. The sergeant questioned me as to why some push ups would affect me in this way. He asked if I worked out before the start of the academy? I said that I had. (I remember the lesson from Middle School wrestling). I couldn't figure it out myself. I knew that the room was hot, and the events were stressful, but I have never experienced anything like that before. It would be several hours later that I would have my answer. While sitting in class, the effects of a virus became evident as I began to get the shakes. But with all of that said, I got through the first day of the academy.

The Baltimore County Police Academy was known to be academically challenging. We lost several recruits who couldn't pass the academic work. Having said that, my biggest concern was the physical training. They pushed us to give one-hundred percent but I always felt to need to hold just a little back. This came in handy when we received an AA session at the end of our regular gym class. There we were doing dying roaches, crunches and other methods of torture. I also remember to this day a statement by our PT instructor. He was referring to our involvement in a foot pursuit. He said, "What are you going to do with them if you catch them?" That was confirmation to me that you always better have some gas in the tank if you are doing police work in the field.

Graduation came in April of 1988. The ceremony was held at a high school in Timonium, Maryland. As the seventy-sixth Recruit class marched into the auditorium, members of a community choir sang the Battle Hymn of the Republic. I was shocked to hear such a Godly song at a government affair. To this day whenever I hear it, I am reminded of that graduation day and the culmination of my preparation to serve.

Chapter 6:

The Early Years

o o o

During the last month of the Police Academy, we were asked to submit our wish list of station assignments. I didn't know much about Baltimore County, so I listed the closest stations to my residence in Harford County. The closest one to me was the Essex Station. Due to my high academic standing at graduation, I was going to Essex.

Essex was located on the eastern end of Baltimore County. It was very blue collar with many residents who worked in the nearby steel plants that were largely closed or reduced at this time. Therefore, there was high unemployment, drug abuse, domestic violence, and despair. The community was predominantly white, and some would call it redneck. There were few minority officers assigned to work there. I would learn all of this later.

My first patrol shift was the dayshift on a Sunday morning. I thought that would be the best day of the week to begin learning the streets. My shift began at six AM. I arrived at the station at five fifteen AM. I was greeted by a Desk Officer. He told me that my shift does not start until eight AM so, therefore, I should go and have breakfast and come back later. I thanked him for the advice but said I have a magazine to read and I'll be just fine. Officer Sheila Farley was on my shift and she was the first one to genuinely greet me and make me feel welcome.

The Essex Station had about one hundred officers assigned to four patrol shifts. I trained on shift 4. There were no other African Americans on that shift. So, on the first day my Sergeant Wayne Clement approached me and said, "When your FTO arrives, you both will be responding to a homicide scene that occurred overnight". My FTO was Lenny Taylor and that's how we spent my first day on the job.

One of the most dangerous communities in Essex was the Village of Tall Trees. This forty-acre complex was built in the 1940's to house civilian defense workers during World War II. The complex was made up of 105 red brick apartment buildings on three streets: Rittenbacker Rd, Doolittle Rd, and Seversky Court. After the war, many residents moved farther out into the suburbs and the community descended into drugs, gunfire and other crimes. With all the ills of the community, this was a great place to learn police work.

After completing five weeks of field training, I was transferred to Shift two, a very laid back place to work, and reported to Sergeant Jerry Foracappo. There were two other minority officers on that shift, my fellow classmate Sylvia Ready and Norman Wesson. The shift was broken down into three squads, and the three of us were each on a different squad. I had heard of racial balancing, which was a term used back in those days. In other words, the Commander spread out the minority officers over the shifts and squads as best as possible to obtain the desired effect of diversity.

This wasn't a huge problem for me because I was used to being a minority in the workplace. I was there to do police work and not overly socialize. I had slowly heard some of the stories of how minorities in the community had been treated in years gone by in the Essex Station. I spent five years in the Essex Station and when it comes to race, two incidents stick out in my mind. Both came near the end of my time or even after my time. The first was when I was working the fire works detail at the neighboring station during the Fourth of July. A white officer walked up to me and said, "It is a shame how some of those officers treat blacks in Essex." I replied to him that I had not noticed much of that. I'll never forget the look on his face as he shook his head. He then said, "They don't do it in front of you!" I didn't know what to say. *What have I been missing and what has been going on all around me?*

The second incident occurred many years later, when one of my former partners mentioned that some redneck officers harassed him for being my friend. I had never known this was occurring at the time and I am grateful to Officer Tony Taylor for ignoring the ill-treatment and continuing to do his job.

With this in mind, I understood the management philosophy of racial balancing to help minimize the bad behavior among the rank and file. As the years went on, the Baltimore County Police Department continued to professionalize and hold officers accountable for their actions.

Satisfied that I had discovered my career calling, I prayed and asked the Lord to direct me to my life partner. A mutual friend, Daphney Gwynn, took a group of singles from our Church in Harford County to the urban center in Baltimore City to visit a storefront church where her friend, Kim Stanley worshipped. That Sunday morning, Kim was singing in the choir. Daphney later invited Kim out to the county to some of our events. One Saturday, I called Daphney at her home. She wasn't home, but her house guest was and answered the phone. It was Kim. I thought to myself, since Daphney isn't at home, I'll talk to Kim. We talked for several hours, and we discovered that we had a lot in common. Soon we began to date. I met her family and she met mine. In 1989 we were engaged to be married. During one of our visits, I made her watch the police movie, Heavens Heroes. It was the true story about the life and marriage of Des Moines, IA Officer Dennis Hill. Officer Hill was killed in the line of duty and his wife had to remain strong for the kids. As you can imagine, it was a hard movie to watch but it talked about the true-life struggles of being in a police family and I felt that Kim should fully understand what she was getting into.

We were married on November 18th, 1989. Daphney's mother sang at our wedding. During the reception, I had to briefly jump into police mode. Our reception was held in the Hall of a volunteer fire department. One of the guests, a good friend of my mother, stepped off the curb and broke her ankle. It was a compound fracture...nasty. So, in my white tux, I directed someone to call an ambulance while I kneeled to comfort her and keep her from going into shock. Most of the guest inside were not aware of the excitement outside. I then returned to the reception.

In 1990 we had our first son Jerome and in 1993 we had our second son William. We continued to live in Harford County as I worked in neighboring

Baltimore County. I only recall one time nearly running into someone I had arrested while I was shopping in our community grocery store. I left the store before being seen by the former arrestee. I have always felt more comfortable living outside of the jurisdiction where I work. Some cities have residency requirements but that is short-sighted, and it ignores the safety of the officer's family.

As a new officer, it wasn't uncommon to have to work weekends and holidays. I found this to be true on my first Christmas morning. Prior to Christmas Day, the Lord impressed upon me to go to the Dollar Store and buy 4 matchbox cars. I put each one in a brown paper bag, stapled it closed, then went to work on Christmas morning. My patrol beat covered the Village of Tall Trees. I saw several kids milling about as I drove around. I would pull up in my marked patrol unit and ask them what they got for Christmas. Most named a little something and I said, "That's nice," and moved on. Then, I made a left turn down the ally of Doolittle Rd. Halfway up the alley I saw three boys standing around. I pulled up next to them and asked what they got for Christmas. I'll never forget what happened next.

One of the boys dropped his head and said, "Nothing, our parents can't afford toys." I said, "Really, I might be able to help with that." As I looked between my bucket seats where the four packages were stored, I grabbed them and noticed that there were now four boys standing next to my car. I do not know where the fourth boy came from. I then handed the boys the packages and told them that it wasn't much. Their eyes got wide and they thanked me as they ripped open the packages to find their Christmas gift.

As I drove off, I felt the Lord whisper to me, "Pay attention to what just happened here. I can use you in this career if you let me."

It was a warm spring night with light drizzle and fog in the air as I begin my tour of duty on the night shift. Not long into the shift, we heard the "Bat Phone". This was the unique sounding telephone that the call taker used to alert the dispatcher of a priority call that was too urgent to send in the normal fashion of a written message. So as the Dispatcher is broadcasting her routine matters and we hear that phone ring in the background, the dispatcher usually said, "All units stand by taking a call". This is usually followed by an eerie pause on the radio and then the emergency tones.

After three tones the dispatcher called my car number and a backup unit for a stabbing that had just occurred on Rickenbacker Road in the Village of Tall Trees. We both responded as well as our supervisor and additional officers.

I was the first to arrive and I observed the victim laying on the sidewalk in the light rain. I asked him who stabbed him, and he told me, Mason. The medics soon arrived and called for a life flight helicopter. Unfortunately, the copter was down because of the bad weather. The victim, Brian, was driven by ambulance to the nearest hospital.

My investigation lead to the full identity of Mason and I obtained a warrant for his arrest. Over the next week, we hunted for Mason. One day on day shift, a tipster told me that Mason was in his grandmother's house in the Tall Trees. I asked for several units and we surrounded the house. After the house was secure, we contacted the grandmother and she allowed us the search the house. We worked our way upstairs and searched each room.

The last place I looked was a small space between the bed and the wall. He was hiding there. He was then placed under arrest and taken to the station and interviewed. He admitted to the stabbing and said it was a drug deal gone bad. He was the seller and Brian was the buyer.

Even though the victim, in this case, was wrong for buying drugs, he was almost killed for no legitimate reason. I kept in contact with the victim and prepared him for the court process just like I was taught in the police academy. This case was an eye-opener for me. As I stated before, Essex was a low-income blue-collar section of the county. The Circuit Court where this felony crime was going to be held was in Towson, the county seat. I picked up the victim and drove him to court. I loaned him one of my clip-on uniform ties, so he would look more presentable. The case was heard and the career criminal who almost killed Brian got a slap on the wrist. I soon realized that where my victim was from played a roll in the outcome. Both suspect and victim were white and from the wrong side of the tracks. Justice wasn't served that day.

Later that year there was a mix up during a bail hearing and a violent felon was inadvertently released from the Essex District Court House. An arrest warrant was obtained, and the entire patrol command searched for the felon. The detectives passed out pictures of the felon. For several weeks we looked high and low without success. At the end of the week, I was cleaning out my uniform shirt pockets when I saw the picture of the felon. I was about the throw away the picture as I was sure he was long gone. The Lord stepped in again and whispered for me to save the photo. I started to argue that the guy was long gone but I decided to be obedient and save the photo in my pocket.

The next day at work we were about to look for another wanted person. My self, several officers and my shift Lt. were staged on a convenience store parking lot when a vehicle entered the lot driving really slowly. The driver was being nosey. The man in the front passenger seat looked me in the face. I thought, he looks familiar. I pulled out the photo and recognized the wanted felon. I walked over to the Lt. and explained that I know we are looking for someone else but in the car that just drove off is the wanted felon we have been looking for. He said, "Are you sure?" I said yes, "I have his photo." He then said, "well go and get that &*%$!"

The vehicle had headed down a dead-end road. As it turned around and was heading out, Officer Libby and I stopped it at gunpoint and arrested the wanted felon.

The Station Captain was really impressed with the fact that a rookie officer observed the felon and made the arrest. Of course, I knew the truth. If I had not listened to the Lord with respect to the photo, I would have never recognized who he was.

Not long after that arrest, The Captain started a new three-person unit called the Community Action Team or Cat Squad. I was asked to join the new specialized unit. I was almost off my 2 years' probation. This was unheard of in Baltimore County to be assigned to a Specialized Unit while still on probation. God was at work.

The primary purpose of the Essex Station Community Action Team was to address quality of life issues in the neighborhoods. Problems such as noise from neighborhood bars at closing time, public drinking, noisy house parties, and the public consumption of narcotics. These problems would tend to negatively impact the quality of life in neighborhoods. Imagine if you lived near the vicinity of a neighborhood bar and between 1:00 and 3:00 AM, you were awakened to people screaming in the streets when you had to get up and go to work or school in the morning. This was a job for the Cat Squad. After enough people get cited and it is traced to the address of the bar, the County Liquor Control Board would act against the bar and shut them down for a few nights until they could get their acts together.

One of our most challenging establishments was Legions Bar on Eastern Avenue in Essex. While the front of the bar faced a commercial district, the rear of the bar faced a residential community. One of the residents was a frequent complainer of the establishment and our supervisor would send us to address the problem. It was there that I learned to do parking lot rips where we would catch people using drugs in their cars after exiting the bars. When we first started our operations, some of the clients were so blatant as to snort cocaine from the hood of their cars.

I recall one night we observed some violation on the parking lot. As we snuck up in our unmarked car with the lights off. The violator begins to pull off the lot and we turned on our lights in pursuit. I'll never forget seeing that the neighbor, a heavy-set older lady, sitting on her front porch watching the whole thing go down. As we took off after the car, she leaped to her feet and yelled, "Yes!" as if her favorite team just scored the final Superbowl Touchdown. That expression reminded me of what residents endured at the hands of some of the neighborhood bar patrons.

Our team made good use of the alcohol and criminal citations. These violations would end up in court. Some of our fellow officers didn't understand why we wrote so many tickets and on occasion clogged up the court docket, but the Captain loved it. We did see victories from some of our battles, especially the houses. These houses tended to be the place of parties each weekend. Our philosophy was once you got on our radar, why wait for the neighbors to get so upset that they had to call the police? We went to the location of these houses and observed for violations. We did have a noise ordinance in the County and if we observed any violation, we could act.

There was a community called Hawthorne that was full of young people who disrespected others. On one of the first nights we were working in their shopping center at the entrance to the community, a juvenile on a bicycle was harassing us, the police. He could see that we're in uniform in our unmarked car and he kept circling us and acting like a general fool. So, I thought a minute and then realized that he was operating a bike at night without a headlight, a violation of state law. We pulled him over and requested his driver's license. Being under 16 years of age, he didn't have one.

Maryland Motor Vehicle Law allowed our computer to create a driver's license number for a person based on their name and date of birth and that would be their new drivers license number in the future. We created the number then issued him a State Citation and sent him on his way. Within an hour his mother called the station, cursed out the desk officer and informed them that it would be a cold day in *&%$ before they paid that citation. I then learned the root of the child's bad behaviors.

When I first joined the Cat Squad I was the junior man and I worked with Mike Lynch, who would later become the Chief of Police at George Mason University and Chris Wrzosek. After they left the unit my final partners were Tony Taylor and Tim Mullaney. We generally worked Tuesday to Saturday on the evening shifts. Often on Friday and Saturday nights, we would work later to cover the bar closing times. We had a great time and learned to read each other's minds when dealing with subjects on the street.

One night, Tim and I were on the back lot of the Mid Way Bar in Essex dealing with some young people and open containers of alcohol when one of the men whispered in my ear that one of the guys in our presence had a gun. I thought for a moment and couldn't risk tipping him off if I tried to tell Tim what was about to go down. I just trusted that Tim would follow my lead. So, while we were casually chatting with the guys about the alcohol, I drew my gun and pointed it at the suspect telling him not to move. I asked him if he had a gun and he said yes. By asking him I figured I would let everyone present in on why this crazy cop is drawing his gun over a beer. The suspect was arrested and the gun was recovered.

At first, I was a little concerned about leaving patrol after only two years, but I then realized that for the next three years we would be making more arrest and getting involved with more action than if we remained in patrol. Most arrests were made in the evening and early night hours of the day and that is when we worked each week. As members of the Captain's Staff, we were often called upon to assist the detective units with search warrants. It was important to have a uniformed officer present when "breaking into" someone's home so that they know it was the police and not other criminals.

We would also have to station someone out back in case the bad guys decided to flee out of windows or rear doors. In our heyday, we could be involved with multiple back to back warrants in a single night. Most times the warrants were fruitful but sometimes they would come up dry. I recall on a few times when they would come up dry that we would tell the drug detectives that we were going back on patrol and we will show them how to get some drugs. It is hard to imagine but at times we could set up surveillance in an area and could tell that a person or persons were going to use drugs before they did them. We would then just wait, watch and arrest. Dealing with some of the repeat violators that were teenagers made me realize that some of the kids we were dealing with were alcoholics and drug addicts. This began to plant the seed for another approach.

After five years on the job working in Essex, I began to look for new opportunities, so I inter-viewed for a Mobile Crime Lab Detective position. I also took the Corporals exam. I got the job and transferred to the Crime Lab. The most frequent call in the crime lab was to process the scene of residential burglaries. I recall responding to an elderly ladies' home on the west side of the county for a burglary. It was in a very nice but secluded area. I arrived there late at night and processed the scene for evidence.

I noticed a tall stack of books in her living room. She informed me that she lives alone and can no longer sleep at night. Therefore, she stays up all night and reads books so that she can protect her home. I realized the trauma that can be inflicted due to a burglary. It isn't just a property crime or an insurance matter. It is an interpersonal crime of supreme victimization. Many courts today just treat it as a shoplifting offense at the local department store. While it is true that many burglars are drug addicts, the pain and harm inflicted on others can be immeasurable. I would later learn this first hand.

One day my wife Kim had left our home to pick up our sons from school. When she returned home she noticed that the back door was ajar. She didn't enter the home but called the Harford County Sheriffs Dept to respond. She later called me at work in Baltimore County and I responded. The burglar kicked in our back door and stole my off-duty gun that was locked in a footlocker. The first thing he did upon entering the home was to remove a butcher knife from the counter in the kitchen. This all occurred in broad daylight. The investigation was completed, and no arrest was made. We took steps to harden our home.

It was later that I began to realize how much it impacted our sons when one wrote about the burglar in a paper at his elementary school. Here I am a cop, out trying to protect the citizens of Baltimore County and I can't even protect my own home. Frustration turned to anger. I had dreams of him returning while I was home or me coming home and catching him in the act. I am sure you can imagine how those dream scenarios all ended. Then I would have to resign myself to the fact that the Harford County Sheriffs Department wasn't going to be able to solve this crime. I then had thoughts of taking revenge on any burglar that I would come across whether in Harford or Baltimore Counties. Somebody was going to pay dearly for what they had done to my family. Over time I realized that this wasn't a proper response to our crime. I had to let it go and move on. But the experience did give me a greater compassion for the victims of burglary.

Even though I had left the Cat Squad, I was still going to court on some of the arrests we had made. One case was continued on from date to date. When it was concluded, the judge mixed up facts of my case with some other case. When I tried to help him, he didn't want to hear it and ultimately found the suspect not guilty for a crime I watched him commit. I was fit to be tied. Early on in my career, senior officers would tell us not to care about what happens in court, just do our job and leave it to others for what happens in court. That sounds wise and rational, but the reality is that the findings in court was a reflection on your work and I always took it personally.

I responded to the Crime Lab Office for the start of my shift. The Detective that I was replacing muttered something about four people being shot. I thought he was joking and besides, I was still mad as a hornet about court. As I logged on my shift, the dispatcher called my car. She told me to respond to the Farmers Bank on Liberty Road for a robbery / homicide.

Upon arrival, I met with the Homicide Detectives. Several suspects entered that bank in the north-west section of the county and shot four tellers for no apparent reason after robbing the place. I took 108 photos of the scene starting across the street and all the interior of the bank. Two of the bodies were left at the scene. The other two were taken to the hospital. I recall stepping over the bodies to get all the photos and to collect all the evidence that the Detectives needed. That scene took up my entire shift with the help of one other crime lab detective. Looking back on that day I realized that God had allowed my emotions to be temporarily hardened because of what had happened in court before my shift started that day. My emotions were turned off and that allowed me to do my job. The suspects were later arrested and that would be my first opportunity to testify in a capital punishment case.

My assignment in Crime Lab only lasted 6 months before I was notified that I was going to be promoted to the rank of Corporal. After the ceremony, I was transferred to Western Traffic. This assignment was about the farthest from my home in Harford County. I also didn't particularly like traffic enforcement. Most of the officers that I would be supervising had more time on the job than I did and certainly knew more about traffic than I did or cared to know. The final problem with Western Traffic was it was a classic hostile work environment with a twist. Several employees, mostly black, were harassing all the supervisors. I had never seen anything like it.

Not long after arriving, I had walked into the locker room to use the bathroom. Several of the black officers were in there talking. As soon as I walked in, all the talking stopped. I went about conducting my business and left. I then realized that I wasn't one of them, I was a supervisor.

I learned the importance of documentation and dealing with bad behavior. This was no doubt the most stressful job of my 20 years with Baltimore County. Despite the bad behavior, I had some very good and conscientious officers such as Mark Crump and Rich Kesterson. Mark would wash his patrol car every day before going on the road. I also worked with some good fellow supervisors. One was Sergeant Bob Hull. He turned me on to talk radio. Our boss was Lt. Minda Foxwell. I had known her from my days working in Essex where she was a sergeant. She had known many battles being a female officer in the early days of female officers.

One morning while I was still asleep I got a phone call at home. It was from Major Kevin Sanzenbacher. I didn't know him or exactly where he worked in the police department. Like any good officer I wondered if he was with Internal Affairs and why was he calling me at home. He went on to tell me about an opportunity to participate in a program called COP SWAP. Baltimore City and County were each going to send one Officer to Cardiff Wales and the Constables in Wales were going to send two Bobbies to Baltimore to work for 7 to 10 days. I was trying to think in my mind where Wales was....

He then stated that the swap will be filmed for a program that will air in Wales and most importantly, the County will be paying for everything. He needed an answer soon. Kim was out grocery shopping, so I told him that I would let him know very soon. I realized that Kim didn't like to be left alone and was still adjusting to living in Harford County, but this seemed like something that I couldn't pass up as they could have asked any number of people to do it.

When Kim came home, I told her about the call and that I was going to say yes. She took it hard, but it was important for her growth as well.

The plan was for Baltimore City's Detective Nevins and I to arrive in Cardiff Wales and the two Constables would enter on the plane after we exited. The film crew would film the entire thing. So, when we arrived, the commercial airline crew asked everyone to remain seated as we, in full dress uniform exited the plane first.

During the next week, we did several interviews and worked several details. The highlight was the detail protecting Princess Diana as she walked the rope line of the crowd. We were stationed along with other Constables to provide protection. The lead supervisor wanted to make sure that we got a chance to meet the Princess. So, the plan was as she got to where we were on the line, we would turn around from the crowd and shake her hand as she walked by.

As the Princess walked near, we turned around as instructed, but she ignored us and kept walking by. The Supervisor, not to be undone, had us move further down the rope line past her so we could try again. I assured him that is wasn't necessary, but he insisted as he wanted us to be able to meet the Princess. So, we did as we were instructed.

She once again ignored us. I think we did it a third time. Now I knew it was well known about our presence in the country and we did both radio and TV interviews. Our police uniforms were different than the Constables and finally being 6' 3" and Black, I stood out in Wales. After she snubbed us the third time, the Supervisor gave up and it was a good thing that he did because I wasn't going to grovel to shake her hand. At the end of the line, she jumped into her car and left the area.

Oh, I just remembered: on one of her passes by one of her security agents gave me a slight shove out of her way. To me, it was clear that uniformed workers were not in the same class as Royalty and therefore should not expect to be engaged. As soon as her limo left, a TV camera was thrust inches from my face and the reporter asked me what I thought of the Princess. I took a deep breath and said, "Very interesting." I recall something else was printed in the paper.

Overall, it was a great experience and I reflected on the fact that serving in local law enforcement rather than the federal agent job that I wanted has turned out to be a good thing. God knew all along!

Chapter 7:

Mid-Career

o o o

One day while attending a training program at the police academy, Colonel Kim Ward (who was my squad sergeant in the police academy) casually remarked that an assignment in Internal Affairs might be good and I told her I wasn't interested in that. About two years later, I was given the opportunity to join the Regional Auto Theft Team (RATT). This team was made up of detectives from both Baltimore City and Baltimore County. The problem was many car thieves would come from the city, steal a car in the county, and return to the city and were home free. With all the violent crime in the city, car theft wasn't the highest priority. The car theft problem continued to grow into a serious regional issue. Therefore, a grant was obtained and the RATT Squad was started.

The geography was divided into east and west and included the City and County. I was going to be the east side supervisor. This meant that I would have Baltimore City Detectives reporting directly to me as well as their county counterparts. The culture of the two agencies were different in almost every way. While the County Police were much more professional and respected by the community, I learned to respect the hard job of the City Officers who worked in a much more violent setting.

Much of our work playing cat and mouse with the car thieves occurred in the city. I recall participating in two separate felony arrests where I had to pull my gun in the time span of thirty minutes. This job was a lot of fun, but I knew the liability of working in the City was like a ticking time bomb.

Not long after joining the RATT I became aware of some serious performance issues with two of my city detectives. Both were African-American. I wanted to get to the bottom of the issue, but I didn't want to be accused of coming down hard on them as a sergeant from the County. So, I invited the West side Supervisor, a city sergeant, to sit in on all the interviews. I interviewed all my detectives to learn what was going on. They told the truth and it was shocking. The city sergeant agreed that the city detectives, who served at the pleasure of their commanders, had to go. I reported the findings to the RATT Commander and the city detectives were replaced.

Not long after this, I met up with my friend Howard. He then relayed a conversation that he had with Colonel Kim Ward. She asked him what was my problem? I was shocked because I didn't know I had a problem. He said, "You have not been in the military, have you?"

I said, "No." He then informed me that when a superior officer suggests an assignment, it is more than just a suggestion. I then realized that he was referring to the assignment in Internal Affairs.

I then put the word out that I would be happy to go to Internal Affairs. After two years on the RATT, I knew it was time to leave before something terrible happened. Not long after I left, one of my detectives shot a violent suspect. The official investigation waited to see how the community responded!!

That is no way to treat the law or the law enforcers. I was glad to be gone from Baltimore City.

An assignment in Internal Affairs is very important in learning how to hold members of your own agency accountable. I found that most complainants just wanted to be heard and all too often, the street supervisor didn't afford the complainant that listening ear and hence the case ended up in IA.

While assigned to IA, I applied and interviewed to attend the FBI National Academy. I was selected. The FBI National Academy began in 1935 and to date, nearly 42,000 law enforcement professionals from around the world have attended the ten weeks live in program located in Quantico, VA. The movie, Silence of the Lambs, showed actress Jody Foster running on the property of the FBI Academy where National Academy students run. The point of the program was to prepare law enforcement professionals for greater leadership in their agency. At this point in my career, my goal was to become a Police Lieutenant. I was a sergeant when I attended the FBI National Academy.

We were assigned roommates at random. I was told the bed assignments were first come first served. My goal was to get there early and make my selection. When I arrived, I saw my roommate was already there. His back was to the door when I entered. Not knowing where he was from or how he would feel about an African American roommate, the time had come. He turned around slowly and spoke with a southern drawl. His name is Mike Burns and he was from Macon, Georgia, and we got along great. One of the things that the staff told us during orientation is that about ten members of our 250-member class will lose a family member to death while we are in the training. This was based on our age and the age of our parents. Well, it came true, my roommate's father died while we were in the training. This gave me the opportunity to minister God's love to him during that time. He later thanked me and said that God had placed us together for such a time as that.

After graduation from the FBI National Academy, I returned to my job in Internal Affairs. During that time, a friend of mine invited me to his place in Coatesville, PA for lunch. His name was Jack Crans and he was the Director of the County Corrections

Gospel Mission. He was also the Police Chaplain for the City of Coatesville and has served on the National Board of Directors for the Fellowship of Christian Peace Officers, USA. But besides all that he was a mover and shaker and master networker. I did not know why but the Lord impressed upon me to wear a tie to the lunch.

When I arrived at Jack's place, he walked outside to meet me. He then told me that he also invited the City Mayor to the lunch. I knew that Jack was up to something, so I asked him what was going on. He said that he just wanted me to meet the Mayor and wanted the Mayor to meet me....no pressure. During the lunch, the Mayor shared how they needed a Police Chief. While I was flattered, I had fifteen years on the job and wasn't able to retire yet. We continued the conversation. I wondered if I could take a one-year leave of absence from the Department and help them while conducting a search for their next Chief. When I returned to work, I met with my Chief Terrance Sheridan and discussed the possibility. He pointed out some of the problems but in the end, he said he would support my decision. I prayed about it and decided it wasn't a good idea. This was later confirmed by the unexpected death of the Mayor. But having gone through this process planted a seed for senior police management.

During this time, I also took the police exam for Lieutenant. I believe I took it five times over the next five years. I passed it each time, but the door wasn't being opened for a series of reasons.

In 1998 I returned to Patrol in the White Marsh area and soon was back in charge of a specialized unit. It was the Community Outreach Team. On this team I supervised five Outreach Officers, one Juvenile Diversion Officer, one Domestic Violence Detective, one Police Athletic Center Officer, six School Resource Officers, six Business Patrol Initiative Officers, and one Corporal.

I really enjoyed this position and held it longer than any other in my career. I think the main reason was the diversity of functions. We could be involved in an Elementary School Talk in the morning and participating in a drug and gun search warrant later the same day.

Much of what we did involved quality of life enforcement just like on the CAT Squad back in Essex.

One evening while working plain clothes and patrolling one of our troubled neighborhoods, I observed a group of juveniles standing in the middle of the street. As I drove by they barely moved out of the road for me. They obviously didn't know that I was the police. This was the type of thing that would frustrate neighbors in the community. So, as I drove by them I intended to turn around in the shopping center at the end of the road, come back and if they did the same behavior, I would stop and let them know what I thought about their behavior.

When I entered the shopping center I looked to my right and saw a person quickly come around the corner and enter the Pizza Hut Restaurant. As he did he seemed to have put his hand up in front of his mouth. As I continued to drive I saw an occupied vehicle on the parking lot, but it was a work van that was marked on the side. It seemed OK. Then the Lord seemed to say to me, "Pay Attention to the Pizza Hut." So, I turned the car around and sat facing the door of the Pizza Hut.

I couldn't get a good look inside, so I decided to move my car over two spaces when suddenly, the suspect came running out of the Pizza Hut in a full sprint. I thought *that is a clue*. I radioed the Dispatcher that a possible robbery just occurred at the Pizza Hut. I gave a description of the suspect and his direction of travel. It just happened to be shift change in White Marsh. Most of the Officers were at the station. The early car was on the road and could have been anywhere in the District. But as fate would have it, she was on the other side of the shopping center when I called out. The suspect ran to the rear of the shopping center and soon the Officer in unit 912 gave foot pursuit. I drove past where they were headed with the hopes of cutting off his escape route.

As I was flying down the street, the group of juveniles were still loitering in the road. But as my unmarked car was speeding towards them, they jumped out of the road scared for their lives. This gave me some brief satisfaction. There was a break in the row houses, so I cut the wheel to the right, jumped the curb and prepared to enter between the houses. I grabbed my radio and gun. As I got out of the car I noticed that the suspect had rounded the corner and was running toward me. I identified myself, ordered him to stop and get on the ground. He kept approaching. I ordered him a second time to stop and get on the ground. He slowed up but kept coming. He was now about fifteen feet from me.

I then removed my finger from touch index and placed it on the trigger ordering him for the final time to stop. He stopped right in front of me giving me a dazed 1000-yard stare. I then reached up with my left hand which also had my radio, grabbed his shirt and forcefully pulled him to the ground. At this point unit 912 ran up and we placed the suspect under arrest. A quick search revealed a gun in one pocket and $914 in cash in the other one.

The employees never called the police because when our suspect robbed them, he told them that he placed a bomb outside and they had better not call the police. We had him in custody prior to 911 getting a call for service. This suspect had committed a string of robberies and he later confessed to them all. I received the Officer of the Month Award for this capture.

In our mission to improve the quality of life in the White Marsh area, I had heard complaints that students from the Perry Hall High School would gather in the upscale neighborhood across the street from the school and smoke both cigarettes and marijuana before class. One of the things I loved doing was surveillance. So, I gathered some of my young outreach officers and conducted surveillance of the students. I must admit, the students were pretty slick. They would stand in a circle and smoke cigarettes and socialize. The schools were all smoke-free environments, so they smoked off campus. As we watched the group from nearby unmarked police cars, I saw it happen. I asked my fellow officers if they noticed the one kid fire up some pot and they said no. We continued to watch and then they finished and went to class.

I decided to give them a week then reconvene my team and conduct some more surveillance. The students returned to their favorite spot and got in a circle. They began smoking cigarettes and then one lit a joint of marijuana and passed it around the circle. I again asked my officers if they saw what was happening. This time they saw it. Our plan was to pull up and jump out on them. When we did, the person holding the pot threw it to the ground. It was recovered and all denied possession of it. The smell of pot was in the air and all six students were placed under arrest for possession of marijuana.

We again waited a week and set up surveillance. The students moved to a different spot in the neighborhood but we observed them smoking cigarettes and pot. They were again arrested.

On our final mission about a week later, we observed a group of Perry Hall students leave the school property and walk into the neighborhood. This time they went into the nearby woods and once again, they were smoking pot. My team of officers tracked them to their party spot and observed them smoking pot. When me made our move, the suspect holding the pot threw it into the stream as they all tried to flee. We captured the students. A funny thing happened to the pot that was thrown. It landed on a dry rock in the stream bed. It was recovered and the students were charged. I recall one of the boys telling us, "Please just send me to juvenile hall and don't bother calling my father." I asked him why and he said, "Because I was arrested last week and he is going to kill me." He didn't mean that literally.

In Baltimore County, we had a program called JOINS, Juvenile Offenders in Need of Supervision. It was a diversion program that helped address the problems of the juvenile while keeping their record clean. The program was for first-time offenders only. My officer was the JOINS Officer for the station. I personally sent a lot of business his way. The program used the restorative justice model and included a trip to prison as part of the "Reasoned Straight" approach. It was very successful in getting juveniles to see the bigger picture concerning their crimes. It was also a wakeup call to many parents about what was going on right under their noses.

Chapter 8:

The End and
the Beginning

o o o

The year was **2004 and I began my last** assignment with the Baltimore County Police Dept. This assignment was the Administrator for the Auxiliary Police Team (APT). The APT was a group of sworn volunteers who assisted the department with traffic control, parking, and security at events. Eileen was my Assistant Administrator and together we recruited, tested, hired, trained and administered the program.

As the police department was undergoing staffing challenges, they removed Eileen to add an additional patrol position. This forced me to run the program alone. In addition to the above duties, I also had to create policy, investigate complaints, promote members, and conduct training.

One example of a policy change was the fact that historically the team would participate in annual employee drug testing in the month of January. The larger police department had a random drug testing policy. I realized that knowing that you are going to be tested each January isn't a sufficient deterrent to bad behavior. So, I created a random process for our volunteers. It lead to one or two members quickly leaving our ranks.

While I didn't understand it at the time, this position was preparing me to be a Chief of Police for a small department. We had between 30 and 40 volunteers on the team with a rank structure of Officer to Colonel with detachments located in each Police District.

During my last few years in the department, I began to think about what was next in my life. I explored the possibility of a new career field and began attending graduate school for counseling.

One night while attending our monthly board meeting at the Helping Up Mission in Baltimore City where I served on the Board of Directors, a light bulb went off in my head. We were having trouble making money at the Mission's Thrift Store primarily due to mismanagement. So, we decided to hire a professional Thrift Store Manager. What a concept. The thought then hit me, you are a cop, not a counselor.

Not long after that meeting, I ran into Bernie Gerst, the Towson University Chief of Police and retired Colonel from the Baltimore County Police Dept. We were both leaving an awards program when we arrived at the door at the same time. He said hello and asked me when I was eligible to retire. I replied, "2007." He said, "Humm." He then said, "I have a Captain who is retiring in 2007." I then said, "Humm."

That brief encounter planted the seed for campus policing in me. It was still being a cop, but it was going to be different. I began attending training seminars hosted by Security on Campus and the International Association of Campus Law

Enforcement Administrators. I learned that there was a big world out there in campus safety.

In 2007, I applied for a Commanders position with the University of Virginia. I was scheduled for an interview. I wasn't sure what to expect or what might be emphasized during the interview and then it happened. The Virginia Tech Shooting occurred four days before my interview at UVA. I felt I had a roadmap. The interview went well, and I was hired. They agreed to allow me to delay my reporting to VA until I completed my remaining months with Baltimore County PD.

My final day with Baltimore County consisted of an Auxiliary Recruit Class graduation and promotional ceremony. During the ceremony, I handed over the reins to the next Administrator of the Auxiliary Police Team. My wife and I left that evening feeling really good until we hit the parking lot. A man walked up to us on the dimly lit parking lot and said, "Are you, Randy Brashears?" I replied yes, and he served me with the first lawsuit in my police career. The nature of the suit was a volunteer on the team had a difference of opinion about discipline that he had received. It occurred to me that I must have arrested nearly 2000 people in my 20-year career and I have never been sued by any of them. Little did I know that this was the life of a Police Chief.

The following day my family moved to Central Virginia to begin my work in Campus Policing. This job was meaningful in that I began to learn what is important and what isn't important in a campus setting. The cultural difference between Maryland and Virginia was shocking. During my first three weeks on the job, I was assigned to ride with supervisors on each shift to get a feel for the University. I'll never forget one Sergeant saying, "It is a shame that nobody trusts each other around here." I didn't know what he meant but soon learned. Kim and I were so excited to make the move to VA and start the next chapter of our lives. I would soon learn that UVAPD was one of the most toxic work environments that I have ever seen. I prayed for wisdom, insight and began interviewing for other jobs. Each time the door was closed.

One day while working a home football game, I received a page, it was from Johnny Whitehead. He was a retired Colonel from the Baltimore

County PD and the current Chief of Police at the University of Massachusetts Amherst. He told me that there was an opening at the University of Massachusetts Lowell. Ordinarily I wouldn't be interested in moving to New England in the cold, but the situation was so bad at UVA that I was open to moving to the moon.

I applied, along with one hundred other applicants and began the long process. During that time, I had spoken to the Interim Chief Allen Roscoe at UMass Lowell PD. He told me about the department. I told him I would come up and look around. He promised to give the wife and I a tour and he gave us his home and work numbers. On the weekend in question, we arrived in Lowell, MA, I called Allen, there was no answer. I called his other number and again there was no answer. We had an appointment to meet and he stood us up for the entire weekend. I was furious. I thought what kind of man is this, and what kind of University is this. Am I in for more of the same as UVA? My wife wisely reminded me that if I get the job, I wouldn't be working for Mr. Roscoe. I remained in the process.

Chapter 9:

Chief

o   o   o

In February 2010 I was working at UVA when I got the official word about the position in Massachuttes. I typed up my letter of resignation and waited for the right time to hand it to the Chief. I recall attending a meeting entitled Ropes and Signs. This was a yearly meeting in preparation for the University Commencement. Another university commander and I were in attendance. It had nothing to do with the police department and it was all that I could do to stay awake. This was one of the learning lessons of higher education. They love to have meetings and talk. Several hours later we were released, and we headed back to the station.

As we were pulling in, the Chief of Police was pulling out. I stopped him and asked him if he had a minute or was he needed somewhere. He replied he did have a minute and returned to his office. I went to my office and got the resignation letter. I really wasn't sure if he would be happy or sad. So, I walked into his office and closed the door behind me. I told him I had some good or bad news depending on one's perspective. I handed him the letter and he read it quietly. He congratulated me and told me that he would tell the department on Monday. This was a Friday. I thanked him and said that I would like to tell both Captains first and he agreed.

I then left his office and something strange happened. I felt that my head might hit the ceiling in the hallway as such a heavy weight had been lifted that I floated back to my office. After two years, three months and three weeks, my time at UVA had ended and I was headed to New England.

I went North before the family to secure a place for us to live. On my way north, I attended the Annual Law Enforcement Conference at Word of Life in Schroon Lake, NY. Kim and I had been there many times in the past. But this time was special for me. I would soon become a Chief of Police. I wanted some of my friends to pray for me in this new challenge.

The conference ends on Sunday with a large meal before hitting the road. I knew that I would be sleepy making the long drive down I-87 through upstate NY, so I had decided to stay overnight and leave first thing Monday morning. On my way to New Hampshire, I stopped at UMass Amherst to visit Johnny Whitehead and get some last-minute advice from him. When several of his union members realized who I was, they rushed up to me and started talking about some retirement gibberish and how they needed us at Lowell to get our elected officials onboard with their desires. They handed me a pack of papers to take to Lowell. I later gave them to our Union Shop Steward in hopes that he knew what they were excited about. This was my introduction into the powerful employee union centered environment in New England.

I obtained temporary housing in a furnished apartment in Nashua New Hampshire. This was near the state line and only nine miles from UMass

Lowell. Once again, I was in a culture shock. No one spoke to each other in the apartment complex. I had even waved to some of my neighbors only to have them ignore me. Now prior to moving to New England, several friends warned us about this cultural difference and told us not to take it personally. It was just how things are between people who do not know each other. It was just a little difficult when your family is out of state and after work you have neighbors who, not only will not speak to you but will not even return a simple wave.

My public swearing-in day occurred in April 2010 on the steps of the Tsongas Center on Campus. Area police Chiefs and University dignitaries were in attendance. The Middlesex County District Attorney Gerry Leone swore me in. It was a beautiful sunny day and members of my police department were lined up along the steps leading up to the top where the swearing-in took place. They all were wearing the nice UMass French blue uniform. I would learn later that they had to swap and borrow clothing to be able to look uniform. Over time different members of the department were allowed to wear different uniforms and some no longer possessed our basic uniform.

Over the next four years, my command staff and I worked hard to turn that old department into a professional police agency that constantly receives praise from those who once knew what we were like. The D.A.'s Office, the Clerk of the Court, surrounding Police Chiefs, and key managers within the University Community noticed the change and have stated so. God has been good. It didn't come without severe challenges, but the results have been amazing.

Policing on a college campus is community policing at its core. Quality of life issues are paramount. Those years in Baltimore County doing quality of life enforcement and community policing have definitely prepared me for this position. Working at UVA, although difficult, gave me a better understanding of higher ed and how they think. That helped shorten the learning curve in the transition from municipal policing to campus policing.

Chapter 10:

Call to Faith

o o o

I believe God cares about our calling in life, how we serve mankind and provide for our families. But more important than that, He wants to call us into a relationship with Him where we can be sure to spend eternity with Him after our journey is done on this earth. This is the most important calling of all.

Around the age of 13, we attended church on the Aberdeen Proving Ground Military Base. They had a Post Chapel that had both Protestant and Catholic Services. We attended the Protestant Services. There were normally three chaplains assigned from different Protestant Denominations. Even though we were church attendees, we were not followers of Christ. It wasn't until one summer when I attended a Vacation Bible School where the teacher presented the Good News of the Gospel and invited us to respond. I did. I realized that I was a sinner and being good wasn't good enough to go to heaven. I needed a Savior to take the penalty for my sin. I asked Jesus Christ to forgive me of my sin and to save me and He did!

My mother had received Christ about a year before I did. Soon we left the Post Chapel in search of a Bible Teaching Church. We ended up attending Aberdeen Bible Church. During this time, we also discovered Christian Radio. Here we could listen to the best Christian Teachers in the nation. It was a good source of spiritual growth.

The problem with many people in America today is the fact that they believe that all is well with God because they are basically a good person. They can usually think of the people or categories of people who are worse, i.e. the criminals, haters, abusers or people who are just mean. This reminds me of when I was invited to speak at the Fellowship of Christian Peace Officers National Conference in 2014. The topic of my talk was Evangelism. There I laid out the problem of thinking we are good and the question becomes how good do we have to be? Most of us recognize that we are not perfect. No one is, so how close do we have to come to perfection: 50 percent, 70 percent, or 90 percent?

Scripture points out that we are all sinners and have fallen short of Gods mark (Romans 3:23).

The penalty for falling short of perfection is death (Romans 6:23).

But God in his mercy provided us a way to have a relationship with Him (Romans 5:8).

We must declare with our mouth that Jesus is Lord and believe in our heart that God raised Him from the dead, then we too can be saved and have a relationship with God (Romans 10:9).

We have a knack for taking something so simple that a child can understand it and make it very complicated. I like to think of it as a marriage. If someone asks you are you married, you do not say sort of or kind of. You either are or you are not. You have a marriage license, or you do not.

You participated in some sort of official ceremony or not. The same is true with whether you are in a relationship with God. Have you committed your life to God at some time in the past? What do I mean by committed? Have you admitted that you are a sinner? Have you asked for forgiveness of that sin? Have you asked God to save you? Have you agreed to allow Christ to be the boss of all the areas of your life?

That is what I mean by a commitment to Christ. Scripture says that it is by grace that we have been saved, not of our own works but a gift from God (Ephesians 2:8-9). Unfortunately, many people want to rely on or trust in being good, being religious, being spiritual, or being moral to put them in a right relationship with God. So, the big question is are you going to trust in your own goodness or put your faith and trust in the one who died on a cross for your salvation?

Something to think about.

Chapter 11:

Connecting the dots

o o o

Examine your past

When you think about the events of your life, do you see any clues that God may be directing you in a certain area? When you played as a child, did you act out being in a certain profession or dream about being a _____?

As I looked back over my life, I wondered why did I have an interest in being a school safety patrol in elementary school and why did I dream about busting shoplifters at the local convenience store? Why did that teacher in middle school select me to take the hoodlum to the office? Why did having the visit from the Natural Resources Officer on career day inspire me to a possible career in law enforcement? Why did Fran tell me about Law Enforcement Exploring? These questions point to a plan that was being laid out for my life before I was aware of the plan. What things have happened in your life that may point to a plan or roadmap to your calling?

Examine your Passion

After spending several hours on patrol with the Aberdeen Police Department, I had a strong passion for policing. I couldn't think of anything else that I wanted to do. What are you passionate about? What job would you almost be willing to do for free provided that your living expenses were covered? I felt that way when I was a summer cop in Ocean City. I would have done it for free, just throw in 3 hots and a cot. Where is your passion?

Examine your Prospects

Do you have the aptitude to live out your passion? Do you want to be a rock star but can't sing or play an instrument? Do you want to be a school teacher but have no ability to obtain a college degree? I find that many young people today do have the ability and education to perform any number of careers, but they do not know what they are passionate about. Some even graduate with a four-year or six-year degree and do not know how they would like to use it, if at all.

Here are some things to consider:

- Your gifts are not just for you, but they may be for the world to use.

- Don't fear failure.

- Listen to the still small voice inside.

- Don't fret about the future, deal with the present.

- Try different things.

- Find the solution to a problem and you might find your calling.

- Don't be afraid to change your mind.

- Seek the advice of others.

- Your calling can change as you go through different stages of life.

I believe the first step is to seek a relationship with the God who made you. Then ask him to reveal your past, your passions, and your prospects to finding that true calling on your life. As a young adult, I had a favorite spot to go to get quiet and hear from God. It was in the Susquehanna State Park. Before major decisions in life were made, I would go to my spot and pray to the God of the Universe for direction. When is the last time you got quiet before God? No earphones or iTunes, or background noise to distract you. You never know, as you begin a search for God, you just might connect some dots and find your calling in life. If you are already in a relationship with God then you realize that our ultimate calling is to love God and love others. By doing this He may lead us to our place of fulfillment and impact on the world around us. Now go for it!

CPSIA information can be obtained
at www.ICGtesting.com
Printed in the USA
FFHW010307181218